I dedicate tl

Adopted .

and the mothers who gave their children up for adoption, whom I believe gave and received them as a result of love.

Ida Mae, my mother, who loved me unconditionally.

Hazel, my mother-in-law, whose memory we honor.

Lezah, my daughter, whom I love unconditionally.

Cover and Interior Design by Katanni Bramhan

ISBN 9-780578-803234

A Note From the Author

Before I even get started, sidebar, I'm not good with exact dates. I may quote the correct year, however, the day, a week and or a month may be off. Now with that being said, here we go.

Special thanks to:

Abba Father, thank You.

Edwin, my beloved husband and Lezah's dear dad - thank you, for everything you do.

All the prayer warriors (my friends) - thank you, for your prayers throughout the adoption process and to this day.

All Lezah's aunties, uncles, and godparents – thank you, for your love and support over the years.

Brenda Brown – thank you, for your patience and a listening ear.

Chris Sedlak – thank you, for pouring into Lezah and teaching her the importance of advocating for herself.

April Battle – thank you, for taking time out of your busy schedule to edit and critique this labor of love.

How do I say "thank you" to the one who God chose to carry my daughter in the womb?

Lezah's birth mother – thank you, for allowing God to lead.

Hazel Backwards
by
Michaia Brown

DIVINE INTERVENTION.

It all started after four years of marriage and not being able to conceive on our own that my husband and I began to pray for the pitter patter of little feet to bless our home. My husband is a pastor, my mother was a prayer warrior, all my sisters love God, and together we all believe in the power of prayer. I learned early on, by watching and hearing my mom pray and, also, testify about the goodness of the Lord, that prayer is a powerful, reliable and necessary tool while journeying through this path called life.

Soon after I began to pray, I was in bed one night reading. Before lying down, I had a talk with God with regards to blessing our home with a child. When I went to rollover to turn off the lights and close my eyes for the night, I noticed a red pencil lying on my nightstand. I looked at it because I never noticed a red pencil before in my bedroom and wondered where it came from because it was only the two of us (me and my husband) in the house. I nudged my husband and asked him if it was his and he said "no." I picked up the pencil and noticed it had writing on it. The writing was the name of an adoption agency with a phone number. I said "wow" and thought is this a sign from God? Really, that quick?

The next day my husband and I had a serious discussion about perhaps adopting. We had previously gone to the doctor and were considering several options to get pregnant and then this. We had never even considered adoption, but after much more prayer and discussion we decided that adoption was the route we would take. The Bible talks about taking care of the widows and the orphans. Therefore, we felt strongly that this was the path God would have us travel.

After several weeks had gone by, we made an appointment with the agency. We had a productive meeting. We were asked and answered many questions. We filled out loads of paperwork. We took care of all the particulars (background check, fingerprinting, and so forth) and finally the home visit. The final appointment was in February of 1996 when we received an approval and were told to sit by the phone and wait for a call saying "we have a boy or a girl." We really hadn't decided which gender we preferred, however, at that particular moment, I believe the boy had a slight edge if we had to choose.

Meanwhile, as the months went by, we went about our daily lives waiting and anticipating the news of the arrival of pitter patter of little feet in our home. Our family and friends were just as anxious and were cheering us on waiting patiently with us. I thank God for all the support we received during this time. And then, in July (5 months in) the call came. "Hello, this is Ms. Soinso, we have a baby girl for you and your husband. She is about a week old, she is beautiful, her mom has struggled with drugs and there is a possibility if and when she cleans up her act the child will be returned to her biological mom." I immediately called my husband and relayed to him exactly what was said to me and unfortunately, or perhaps fortunately, we both decided that this particular child would not be the best child for us. We did not want to expose ourselves to a situation where we would fall in love with this child and vice versa, or become emotionally attached and then the child is snatched from our home. We felt that would be harmful to the child as well as to us. Therefore, we called the agency back (after much prayer and discussion) and told them we would prefer to wait for a more stable opportunity to present itself. No guilt, no shame, just certain we made the right choice.

We went about the summer months enjoying one another trusting soon and very soon we would have a new addition to the family. The summer rolled over into fall, still no word from the agency. Meanwhile, sadly, in October, my husband's mother died unexpectedly. Needless to say, it was a sad time for us and the entire family. We both have a decent number of siblings, he has four siblings and I have five. As we gathered together making arrangements and sharing stories about our loved one and preparing for the funeral, we quietly thought about adding to the family and knowing he or she would never meet Grandma Hazel. Yes, my husband's mom's name was Hazel. Hazel was a beautiful spirit who loved her children and grandchildren with every fiber of her being. She doted on those grandchildren with love, hugs and smooches. Grandma Hazel was an excellent cook and loved to feed us all. She would have special surf and turf dinners for everyone's birthday. I remember the first time I spent Christmas at her house and those grandchildren would have boxes upon boxes piled up all around them. Patiently, we sat while each person took the time to strategically open each gift slowly and carefully with a huge smile on their face. Grandma Hazel was a loving, caring, wife, mother and grandmother who knew how to make each person feel like her favorite. I loved her and still miss her to this day. I thought to myself, unfortunately our baby would never get to meet their paternal grandmother. The thought saddened me.

About a week from Grandma Hazel's passing and maybe two or three days after the funeral my husband and I received another call from the adoption agency, again, which went like this, "hello, we have a baby girl for you and your husband. She is about a week old, born on October 23, the biological mother did not smoke, drink or do drugs. She said she is just unable to take care of another child right now. The adoption will be sealed. She just wants her little girl to be placed in a loving home." Tears welled up in my eyes and I felt this is the call we have been waiting for. This was God's perfect timing. Wow, the family was still mourning and they could use some good news. I was so excited because I knew deep in my spirit that we were about to become the parents of a beautiful baby girl. I reached out to my husband, told him the wonderful news and when he came home we decided we would call the agency the next day and say "yes" we want to meet this beautiful little girl who we were sure we would bring home.

The next day, we reached out to the agency, set up the appointment and realized it was exactly nine months later from the day we had our first meeting. In addition to that, her birthday was the day after the passing of her grandmother (my husband's mother) and I already had purposed in my mind that I would tell her grandma was going up to heaven and you were coming down from heaven and I'm sure you locked eyes on one another along the way. My husband and I were elated, the meeting went great, and we shared the news with the entire family. Everyone was thrilled!

THE NAME PLAN.

In the meantime, our daughter needed a name. After meeting with the agency, it took about a month before she came to live with us. It was right after Thanksgiving and before Christmas. I told you all about me remembering dates. However, the bedroom was done, the walls were painted, crib made up, stuff animals all over, and everything gender neutral. Although, the room was nice, I now knew we would be bringing home a baby girl. In the back of mind I knew that the entire scheme would be changed before she could walk. While anticipating the call from the agency to come pick up our daughter, I was sitting in her room thinking about a name. I had thought of several names in combination of mine and my husband's name together. However, I always liked the name Imani (which means faith). The scripture reads "faith is the substance of things hoped for the evidence of things not seen." In that moment the scripture came alive and I knew her middle name would be Imani. Then I thought about the fact that since we have a girl perhaps I should pay homage to my mother-in-law. But I just was not feeling the name Hazel. Hazel Imani and Imani Hazel together didn't ring any bells for me. So then I took the letters from h a z e l and mixed them up and finally turned them around and there staring me in the face were the letters l e z a h and a light bulb went off and I started smiling and I said "that's it Lezah…Lezah Imani Brown!!!" "That's it" I shouted to my husband, "our daughter's name is Lezah" – hazeL Backwards.

THE DAY.

December 12, 1996 is here. The day we go to the agency to pick up our baby girl has arrived. The day we would meet her face to face is today. The day we get to hold her in our arms has come. God is so good. Yep, as we drove, we talked and anticipated what it would feel like when we laid eyes on her. In the back of my head, I could hear God whispering "I heard your cries." I thought, not just my cries God. I had my prayer partners, dear friends, praying with us. Yes, God is so good. We serve a prayer answering God. He knows all things and He knew what my husband and I needed and He knew what the family needed at this time. Our, baby girl, Lezah was going to bring us all so much joy.

We finally made it to the office. I was feeling every emotion, joy, peace, love, happiness, etc. I felt tears in my eyes and I know they were tears of joy, but they were also tears of apprehension. Like, am I going to be a good mother? Is her father going to be a good father? Is she going to like us? Will she love us? What type of personality would she have? Will she have a relationship with God? So many questions stirred up in my mind, but as we walked in the door of the office and the woman asked us to sit, I realized all things are possible with God and we can do all things through Christ who strengthens us.

As we sat, we could see out of the corner of our eyes a bundle of joy coming toward us in the arms of one of the employees. As they drew closer to us, we stood up and the woman placed our baby girl in my husband's arms. She didn't cry or anything, she held her head up and then as he embraced her she relaxed her head on his chest. Of course, the tears flowed and we both looked at her and said "hello." We had a brief discussion about her former care givers and were handed a book and a note about her likes, dislikes and habits. The Adoption Book, is what they called it, had pictures of her as a newborn, a bio regarding her birth mother amongst other little things. It was suggested we use the book as a tool when we had the conversation with her about the adoption. We thanked all those involved one hundred times over, wrapped her in a beautiful pink fluffy snowsuit, covered her in a pink blanket, and walked out the door towards the car. We are on our way home. We are family.

While walking to the car we were smiling, singing and feeling forever grateful. As we placed her in the car seat I climbed in the back with her as my husband drove. It seemed like a long drive home, but I was glad to examine her from head to toe. Finally, we pulled up into our driveway. At the time, I operated a daycare in my home, and most of the parents kept their children home that day except one. As we walked in, my little client was there along with two of our dear friends, who agreed to watch the little one while we picked up Lezah. However, while we were away, they decided to decorate the house with balloons, toys, gifts and new baby essentials. It was a blessing to see others sharing in our joyous occasion. They, too, proceeded to examine her from head to toe, checking her fingers and toes and giving me instructions on the dos and don'ts of newborns and toddlers. They both were seasoned parents and I welcomed every bit of their instructions.

That evening, the house was filled with family. All her aunties, uncles, cousins, extended family, Grandma (my mom) and Grandpa (my husband's dad) were there to meet her. In that moment, I looked at my beautiful baby girl, listened to all the cooing, the laughter, the comments, and knew she would be spoiled with a capital S...and also knew in that moment we were meant to raise a girl. God doesn't make any mistakes.

After all the company left, and the house quieted, my husband and I had an opportunity to breathe and take it all in. Lezah was the catalyst that God used to bring joy and laughter to my husband's family (after their recent loss) as well as to my family and the world. Yes, I know that sounds grandiose. However, we serve a God who made us all for a purpose. We realized ours when we became parents. I'm living another as I write this book. One of the many golden nuggets I will purposely share with Lezah over the years. We, too, were being used by God to let her know she was not a mistake. She was born with purpose, for a purpose on purpose.

We wiped her down. I placed her in her kimono. By the way I love kimonos. Whenever one of my sisters would bathe one of my nieces and/or nephews, and put on their kimono, that was one of my favorite things to see them run around in. Now here I am, a mother, dressing my own baby girl, Lezah, in a kimono. I couldn't wait until she began to walk and run around in one. It's amazing how the little things can bring you joy. We placed her bassinet, next to our bed, and our baby girl slept all through the night.

GRANDMA KNOWS BEST.

I remember calling Grandma (my mom), who we referred to as Grandma since her first grandchild was born, early the next morning and she asked "how was she through the night?" I responded "she slept straight through the night." My mom replied "she's home." What a great feeling that was to hear her Grandmother say "she's home." A mother knows what a daughter needs to hear when she needs to hear it and I needed to hear that. I thank God for the nuggets He allowed my mother to drop in my spirit over the years.

I'm grateful she still has one grandma around to shower her with love, hugs, kisses and words of wisdom. I didn't have the luxury of knowing either of my grandmothers. When I met my mom's mother she was well up in age and in a nursing home. Although I never experienced that type of love and affection for myself (from either of my grandmothers), I was blessed to watch that relationship develop between my mom and daughter. Lezah really loved Grandma and I didn't know just how deep until I ran across something she wrote after God called Grandma home in 2007. However, I should have realized it when she (at nine-years-old) did not hesitate to pay tribute to Grandma by dancing for her during her 80th birthday bash. You see Lezah is more of a behind the scenes girl, but when we asked her to dance she stepped up to the plate.

December 1996 was a great month. The month Lezah came to live with us. The month our family grew. Lezah's first Christmas. You would not believe the amount of gifts our baby girl had under the tree. Boxes were piled high and clothes, clothes and more clothes on both the couch and the loveseat. These blessings were from family and friends. It was also the first night she spent with Grandma, without us. Prior to her coming home my husband had bought tickets for a show at Radio City to see an illusionist. I really didn't want to leave her, but I knew it was a great opportunity for her to bond with my mom. As it turned out, we had a great time and so did they.

LOVE ON DISPLAY.

Meanwhile, in late January 1997 some of the members of the church we attended at the time along with her intended Godparents gave us a baby shower. While I thought Christmas was over the top, you had to be there to comprehend what transpired at this baby shower. Along with the many gifts, was so much love, laughter and advice. I give all the glory to God because our daughter lacked nothing. She received so many memorable and practical items. I used this opportunity to write her a letter revealing how much I loved her. Many letters would follow over the years.

He (God) placed people in our lives who accepted our daughter for who God purposed her to be, a beacon of light and of hope to those less fortunate. With that being said, there are always one or two who don't or won't get it. I do remember one person (from the church) who said to me (after she was born and placed in our home) "I'm praying God will give you and your husband a real baby." However, in that moment I realized my purpose was to be a mother and a godly example to my baby girl and not get caught up in nonsense. Therefore, I just smiled and kept it moving because God did give us a real baby and her name is Lezah – hazeL Backwards.

As the months went on and we watched her grow, I experienced a love I never experienced before. We are conceived in our mother's womb and we are blessed to feel love from the second we are formed. We enter the world and for the most part there are two people (parents) who immediately shower us with more love. We feel love from extended family members. We grow and meet friends and experience another type of love. We become grown up (or think we are grown up) and meet someone of the opposite sex and are attracted and boom we are in love. And, God willing, that love will cause us to get married, be blessed to have a child or children and become entwined and entangled in love, love, love and more love.

What I'm trying to say is "love is forever evolving." There are all types of love we will experience while on this journey called life. Welcome it! Embrace it! Love it! The love I feel for my baby girl is different from the love I feel towards my husband. Although, different, but equal, they are both loved. Many of you can understand what I'm saying. Also, even though she didn't come from my womb I can't imagine loving her any more or any less. The love I have for my baby girl is unconditional and I thank God for her. But know this, I don't love her, my husband or anyone else more than I love God our, creator. God is love. I love Him because He first loved me and because He loves me I can love others. Another nugget I shared with my daughter is that although God did not form you in my womb, God formed you in my heart and that love is our bond.

In the meantime, our days were filled with joy and laughter. Between being a mother as well as a caregiver, I learned to juggle and find enjoyment while doing so. I'm fortunate to have a daycare in my home and a new baby added to the mix of five other little ones that I truly adored. The daycare which I have been operating in my home for the past two or three years prepared me for motherhood. I always loved children and desired to be a mom since I was a teenager. I remember my mom saying to me once "I hear you talk about having a baby, but I never hear you talk about getting married or finding a husband. You know those two things go together." I used to just chuckle. However, in all honesty I knew for sure I wanted to be mother. Truthfully speaking, I was never sure I wanted to be a wife. I guess that's why I didn't get married until my early thirties and I was forty when God answered my prayers and blessed our home with a beautiful baby girl. One thing I know for sure is that His timing is always the right time.

14

SHE'S YOURS, LORD.

February 16, 1997. This was the day we chose to have our baby girl dedicated back to God. Wow, the idea of standing at the front of the church, all the family surrounding her, along with the pastor and three sets of godparents brought tears to my eyes. A baby dedication and/or christening is important to our family. My husband and I have about five godchildren of our own. Choosing godparents should be well-thought-out and prayed about. You see, for me, a godparent is not just someone who will buy this or that for a child...a godparent to me means someone who will be there if something should happen to one of the parents, whether through a job loss, sickness or death. Then the godparent should be there to pick up the pieces whether spiritually, physically, emotionally and or financially. I thank God for those we chose for our daughter and they are a support system for her to this day and I have no doubt they will be there for Lezah whenever she needs them.

The service was beautiful and spirit filled. Afterwards, the family and friends gathered at our home for dinner and desserts. We took loads of memorable pictures with Grandpa, Grandma, the godparents and Lezah laughed and smiled through it all. Love permeated the rooms and I could feel my heart beat as tears of joy rolled down my face. I guess you know by now I cry a lot since God answered our prayers. When I look at her, think of her and imagine the plans God has in store for her, yes, I still cry.

WE ARE FAMILY.

We've had several memorable moments watching this little one grow, but the next big one was the day the adoption was finalized. August 1, 1997. She was not quite ten months old yet. We all woke up very excited, even Lezah. I believe she, too, knew this was the day we would officially become a family. "HALLELUJAH!!!" We dressed her in a beige and white plaid dress paired with beige shoes and white socks with laced fringes. Her hair was picked out into a curly afro with a cute white beret placed on the side. My husband and I wore our Sunday best as we wanted to present ourselves well before our lawyer and the judge. Our sisters, her aunties, and her godparents were all in attendance. It was a blessed day all around. We all gathered together in the court room and the judge asked a few questions and Lezah looked around the big room in amazement. It was surreal. This is a defining moment in all of our lives. I could feel the presence of God all around us. After the official proceedings were complete, we all returned to my home, enjoyed one another and inhaled and exhaled while taking it all in. Our family was completed the day the woman at the agency placed our baby in my husband's arms, however, this day gave us closure. We had adoption papers signed by a judge to accommodate the birth certificate with our names listed as parents and her name on it - Lezah (hazeL – backwards) Imani Brown.

It is during times like these wherein you are forced to acknowledge that God knows everything and we know absolutely nothing. In these precious moments we trust that God has a plan for us. According to scripture, the plan is to prosper us and not to harm us, plans to give us hope and a future.

GROWING UP LEZAH.

It was a warm sunny day and my house was a little quiet because I would close the day care down for the last two weeks in August to re-group and enjoy my family. My sister (her godmother) was visiting and baby girl was pushing her walker around the living room and then she kind of fell backward. Lezah preferred to walk while pushing the walker for support instead of sitting inside the walker. However, before I could get to her she picked herself up and began taking steps on her own without holding on to the walker. I said to my sister, "oh my God she is walking." (Or maybe she said it to me). Either way, our baby girl was walking at ten months old.

Before we knew it, September was here, day care back in session, school back in session and you could feel fall in the air. Next month, we celebrate Lezah's first birthday. Wow, how time flies when you are having fun. Now I had to think about planning her first birthday party. Since she is only turning one and she doesn't really understand the concept, I decided to do something in my home and keep it simple and that's what I did. I invited a few friends and family. However, the big thing was her hair. Lezah was born with a head full of hair. She had a cute curly afro. I would wash it, pick it out and place a beret or a bow in it and keep it moving. My friends decided it was time for me to start braiding it, putting it in pigtails or something. I'm not that mother or that girl. My hair at the time was locked. I never liked doing hair so I called on one of my friends who loved to do hair and did it well. She came over and she braided Lezah's hair for the first time. I was forever grateful and she gave me some pointers on what to do and not to do going forward. We had a great first birthday celebration. I ordered strawberry shortcake (my favorite) because she didn't have a favorite at the time. Lezah looked cute with her hair braided. We also had a scheduled photo shoot and took some memorable shots to hang on the wall.

Going forward I started twisting her hair. I never got the hang of braids and because of her hair texture, the twists were easier and complimented her face. I must say she wore twists until she was about to go off to high school. Hey, what can I say? They were stylish, easy and she wore them well.

I remember one day when she was about four or five year's old and was attending school I was washing her hair and she asked me "what the word adoption meant." Now you have to understand we were told by the adoption agency to tell her early on that she was adopted. They felt that because others knew, such as family and friends, it would be better if we tell her instead of letting her hear it from someone else. In support, my sister gave Lezah a framed poem as a gift about the adoptive mother and birth mother and we would read this poem to her frequently. The poem is still hanging on her bedroom wall. However, we knew she would not fully grasp it until later on in life. On this day, for whatever reason she asked the question and I proceeded to explain the best way I could. She went onto ask "if I carried her in my belly" and I proceeded to say "no." Oh my God, she started crying and screaming and saying "you are not my mother" over and over again. I was in shock and I was in damage control mode all at the same time. I dried her hair, I carried her to the sofa, and I explained how God formed us together in the heart. I told her I loved her, daddy loved her and her birth mother, also, loved her. I told her "she was lucky because she had two mothers that loved her unconditionally." I told her "how me and daddy prayed and God answered our prayers." I explained to her "that I was sure her birth mother was praying too." I went on to say "that when God puts families together it's forever and lasting and loving." That's the day I wanted her to understand more than anything the power of prayer; another golden nugget. In many ways, this was a teachable moment. To this day, I don't know if she fully understood what I was saying or if she was completely satisfied with the answer. I do know she calmed down and we hugged. My goal was to reassure her and give her that sense of security so she would always feel safe. In the meantime, our lives went on but I always kind of felt deep down (a mother's intuition) there would always be a void in her heart that only God could fill. Moreover, I continuously pray for her daily and I often ask God to fill her with HIS love. God fill the void in her heart with YOUR love in Jesus' name.

Growing up with day care in my home, Lezah was exposed to being around others and although, an only child, she knew the importance of sharing. However, when she was three, my husband was called to pastor a church in another city and we moved. Due to the move, I gave up my day care. Once we were settled in our new environment I enrolled our daughter in day care which was housed in a catholic church, reluctantly, but I knew she needed to be with other children. To be honest, I was not happy with the move at first because I loved my church home and my community, however, as time went on we all adjusted. We bought a beautiful Bichon Frese we named Maxi who was great companion for Lezah. We were fortunate to live near a park, a library and nice restaurants. The family, along with Maxi took long walks together, ate out at the sidewalk café and Lezah and I spent quality time at the library.

My husband pastored the church for three years. After we returned to our home in South Orange he was soon called to pastor another church. This time we stayed in our home and commuted to the church which was about twenty five minutes away by car.

OFF TO SCHOOL.

When we returned to our home, I enrolled Lezah in a private school in Newark. From there, she went to a public school. To our surprise, our daughter struggled through school. I say to our surprise because I read to her daily. I would play tapes at night with the ABC's and 123's. She watched Sesame Street on a regular basis along with videos I would buy for the kids when I operated the day care. I believe she was in the 2nd grade when we were advised by one of her teachers to have her tested. I welcomed the suggestion because I knew something was going on once she started getting homework and we both would be at the dining room table crying. She would ask "why am I stupid?" And I would reply "you are not stupid, you learn differently and unfortunately the public school system is not equipped to teach students who learn differently." Yes, that was my response because it was true. I work in the school system and I believe to this day that public schools are not equipped to handle students who learn differently, therefore, we are forced to place a label on our children to afford them the extra help they require. (That's another book). Either way, I did what I had to do to allow my daughter to navigate the school system without feeling less than.

Please don't get me wrong. Some students do need to be classified and my daughter was one of those students who benefitted, particularly, when she went to high school. I can honestly say things turned around for her in elementary school after they pin pointed her needs. However, middle school was a struggle both academically and socially. Unfortunately, I didn't learn she was being bullied in middle school until she was in college. Yes, that's when our daughter informed us that not only was she being bullied in middle school she was also being bullied in church. I said, "church, really?" Yes, by children and adults. I must say it was disheartening and disappointing to learn this, but I wasn't shocked. I have lived long enough to know children can be mean spirited and if mean spirited children aren't checked early on they grow up to be mean adults. Thank God she got through it, however, not without some scarring that is not noticeable on the outside but causes one pain on the inside.

After Lezah informed me about the bullying, I couldn't help but reflect on her early school days and ask "why did we not see this?" Did the bullying affect her learning experience or did her learning disability cause her to become a target for bullying? I realized that you can live in the same house with someone and you think you know all that's going on with them and you know everything about them, but you really don't. She taught me a valuable lesson, people share what they want to share, and our loved ones can be going through and they learn early on how to mask the pain. How do you help someone who doesn't know how to ask for help? How do you help someone who doesn't know how to articulate their true feelings?

Most of us teach our children that school, church and home are safe environments – and then something happens that causes them physical, mental or spiritual harm or pain and they realize they're not safe? How do they move forward? How do you come to the one you trust and tell them this is no longer truth? I beat myself up for a long time about this and I'm just sharing that fact about myself now. In addition to her being bullied at church and school, we also later learned that a family member whom we love dearly was also giving her grief due to jealousy. That, too, really hurt my heart to the core and caused me to question my parenting skills. Why did I not see what was going on with my daughter?

Life is a journey. While on this journey we will experience the good and the so-called bad. However, I know the good always outweighs the bad. Today, I regularly encourage my daughter and my husband by saying, "don't let nothing or no one steal your joy." (My mom used to say that to me when I was having a bad day.) Also, if I may share a nugget with my readers, "please pay attention to your children and when you notice the slightest change in their behavior don't hesitate to ask questions." Furthermore, don't be ashamed to seek professional help.

Moving on, if I must say so myself, my baby girl is beautiful. I'm proud of the way she carries herself and handles herself for the most part. I taught her early on that everybody is not your friend and a friend will be there for you through thick and thin. A friend won't leave you in the trenches and when mom and dad get comfortable with allowing you to hang out and go here and there, always remember those you leave home with are the ones you return with. This is a lesson my mom and older sisters taught me early on. I wanted to instill that in Lezah. Well, she learned while in 7th or 8th grade about who to call friend. Grateful to this day, she is not a follower. Amazingly, she seemed to take it in stride when someone proved themselves not to be who she thought he or she pretended to be.

Over the years she learned how to swim, she played basketball starting in middle school through high school. She was part of the stage crew, although, I always wanted her to be on stage. A momma can dream, can't she? Nevertheless, our girl always liked being behind the scenes. I came to admire the stage crew because they work hard and play an integral part in things running smoothly. I, also, had to learn to respect her choices. I'm still learning that.

Meanwhile, it's time to enter into the 8th grade. Wow, you are now the big girl on campus. Not only that, you are a teenager. Turning thirteen was a little scary for both of us. You know now I have a teenage daughter. And now that teenage daughter is feeling herself. She is about to experience that thing (her cycle) that can cause her to get pregnant if she's is not careful. (I'm laughing while writing this). It's time for the conversation. You know the one about the birds and the bees. The one I never had with my mom. I kind of sort of had it with my sisters. Thank God for older siblings. However, all Lezah has is me. Well Dad, but what is he going to tell her and she does have her aunties, wait maybe this is where one of her godmothers can fill in. (I'm still laughing). Anyways, we had the conversation and I bet if Lezah could tell it we had many, many conversations. She would say "mommy didn't leave any stone unturned and there weren't any birds or bees mentioned."

She appeared to be growing into her own and getting over her fears about being in middle school. She was being a little more social and I think she had a little bit of a crush on someone. I wasn't sure who, at the time, but her dad had bought her a phone for her 13th birthday and I overheard a lot of whispering and giggling. I don't know if I was more excited about her graduation that year or her eighth grade dinner dance. I think she was more excited about the dance. She got her hair fixed nicely. She wore a cute sleeveless dress that draped her chest and her first pair high heels. I loved the outfit and was happy they traveled by bus to and from the venue. We dropped her off at the school, took lots of pics and returned there to pick her up when the bus returned. She said she had a great time and that made my heart smile. I thought Lezah – hazeL backwards – is growing up.

It was a warm summer day and my sisters on both sides of the family, her aunties, and dad gathered together for her graduation from 8th grade. As I sat in the hot auditorium my mind began to wonder. I began thinking about how far she has come from that day they placed her in her dad's arms and she immediately rested her head on his chest. That visual will forever be imbedded in my mind. Then placing her in the car seat and heading home, anticipating a house filled with family and friends ready to greet/meet her. I thought of her taking her first steps, saying her first words and how excited I was when she was potty trained. That was an interesting time because early on (after she learned how to walk) whenever she had to go boo-boo she would go into a corner of a room and squat. At first I didn't realize what was going on. Then after several times watching her and getting a whiff afterwards, it dawned on me she knew to squat when she had to boo-boo. Moving forward when I noticed her in the corner, I began leading her to the bathroom. Needless to say and lucky for us, she learned to boo-boo in the toilet before understanding the concept of pee-peeing in the toilet. But either way it took a load off me. (smiling).

I began reminiscing about every birthday party. The one that stood out the most was when she turned three. We had a party in my basement and she was dressed in a red/white striped polo shirt with a denim skirt and navy blue sneakers looking like a little model. (One of my favorites outfits on her.) All her guests showed up and everyone had a great time. I remembered every birthday, including the one when she shared the birthday party with another friend whose birthday is the day after Lezah's. I believe it was Lezah's 10th birthday, which was fun, at one of the inside amusement parks. They also shared Lezah's 13th and the friend's 12th birthday. That year, we (both families) rented a limo, to their surprise, had their nails done, had lunch at Dave and Busters, and shopped until they dropped at the mall.

Graduations can be a little long and boring even if it is your child is graduating. So, therefore, my mind continued to wander. I thought about the Halloween party she attended at one of my goddaughter's homes in which she dressed as Angela Davis. I picked her hair out into a big afro and she wore jeans with a black turtleneck...so cute. We even managed to get a picture of her with hand balled into an I'm Black and I'm proud fist.

I even had time to reflect on the many vacations we shared to date. Lezah can say she has traveled the world by age 13. (Laughing while typing). We have many memorable vacations. I believe her first vacation was at two- years-old when my side of the family traveled to Las Vegas. She was in a stroller and my husband kind of got stuck doing all the baby sitting because when I'm with my sisters I try my best to hang out with them every opportunity I can get. Then at three, we traveled to Paradise Island in the Bahamas. That was a great time! I remember how much she enjoyed the white sand beach and the beautiful blue/green water. At four, we went to Georgia to attend my husband's family reunion. Oh what a time, what a time. The family was very welcoming and accommodating and I remember the food was the best I have ever tasted. We have spent time with my sister in Colorado. We have gone to Texas to visit friends. At this point, the family has traveled to Disney World on several occasions, to Williamsburg, Pennsylvania, and Virginia Beach. We also traveled Niagra Falls on both the New York and Canada side. Yes, Lezah has done a lot and seen a lot in thirteen years.

Furthermore, I reflected on the many water parks, amusement parks, museums, plays and concerts she has been exposed to. Our favorite spot was Sesame Place. It was something about Sesame Place – we were never ready to leave. I guess her dad and I were still big kids at heart. When raising a child that's definitely a plus. I remember the time we went with three other couples and their children for a weekend. We almost got thrown out of the hotel because the kids were running up and down the halls from room to room making all kinds of noise. Despite a little chaos, we survived and the other guest did too.

I also reminisced about the times she spent with her aunties overnight, particularly her aunt/godmother. She would hang out with auntie and uncle all day, eating, playing, watching television, jumped all over the bed and then have them call me around midnight to come pick her up. Of course, I never gave in or did I? I can't remember at this point in my life. She also, loved her overnight stays at her other auntie's (my youngest sister) house because there she got to spend time with her cousin. Remember she has aunties on both sides that loved spoiling her. Another auntie on her dad's side, who is a teacher, would take her with her on class trips to the zoo and the museum.

We've had memorable Thanksgiving and Christmas dinners in which we shared with both sides of the family. We also had plenty cookouts at her auntie's house in Bayonne and later over the top cookouts in Delaware. She spent lovely outings with her godparents shopping, eating out and going here and there. Can we say spoiled with a capital S. I'm just saying.

Finally, another standout memory (and then I'm going to get back to the graduation) was when my sister (one of her godparents) got married and her soon to be husband stood at the altar holding Lezah (who I believe was two at the time) in his arms. It was a small intimate wedding and watching him wait on his soon to be wife walk down the aisle holding his soon to be goddaughter in his arms added to this sacred, loving festive occasion. We have many blessed memories to share regarding her young life. However, this season is done. She made it through!!!

As they called out her name "Lezah Imani Brown," shook her hand, smiled and said "congrats", tears rolled down my face and I thought God thank You for hearing my prayers. Thank You for blessing my home with the pitter patter of little feet. Thank you for allowing those little feet to grow into big feet. High School, here comes big foot.

HIGH SCHOOL.

Please understand, my favorite daughter, (I can call her my favorite because she is my only daughter) was a little reluctant about high school because I worked at the high school. I told her that attending the school where I worked would be a positive thing, as opposed to a negative. Of course she didn't see it that way at the time. However, once school started, and she began navigating the system she agreed my being there was a plus. Well, for freshman year anyways. Being a freshman in high school can be a little intimidating and my job along with several other secretaries in the office was to try to make the freshman feel welcome and comfortable in their new setting.

Therefore, my fav daughter got the royal treatment. My co-workers took her under their wing and looked out for her. They truly went beyond their call of duty. In the meantime, she adjusted well, knew the floor plan, and more importantly, learned to keep her head above the fray. I must say after freshman year, I was an afterthought. We were like two ships passing in the night. We only communicated during school hours when she needed a few bucks or if a situation arose with a teacher. Otherwise, she maintained a low profile while trying her best to keep up with her academics, along with her sports.

High school was an exciting time for all of us. As I mentioned earlier we got through freshmen year with the help of many. Lezah made friends, joined the basketball team, developed meaningful relationships with the dean, her counselor and her case manager. All three, the dean, counselor and case manager were amazing and attentive. They became her "go to" persons. With their help and expertise, Lezah learned the importance of advocating for herself. Moreover, she blossomed into a well- rounded productive student. The relationships were developed to the point she still keeps in contact with the dean and the case manager to this very day.

I am forever grateful for the wisdom and knowledge they bestowed upon her, as well as the time they spent listening to her. Sometimes as adults we underestimate the importance of just listening. The Bible says "he who has an ear let him hear." I know the scripture is referring to hearing what say the Lord, however, we should implement that principle in our daily lives.

It's amazing to watch your child grow through adolescence (ages 10-19). The process of watching the mood swings, experiencing the hormone changes, sniffing out the crushes and getting wind of the "I know everything and you know nothing phase." It caused me to question myself, reflect on my own adolescent days and grow.

Question? Am I doing all that is required of me as a parent? Reflect! I know I did many things that made my mom want to pull her hair out! Yes, and grow, because the world is forever evolving. As the world progresses our children will develop and mature quicker than we did. The Bible teaches us that they will become more wicked (unfortunately) and wiser. For those who believe (in Jesus Christ) the Bible is being fulfilled right before our eyes. With that being said, we, as parents have to understand the importance of having open dialogue with our children. More importantly, pray over your children daily. And, finally, trust God through the process. Okay, I will not turn this into a sermon. (smile).

I would often say to a friend of mine at work "parenting doesn't come with a book" and she would always reply "yes it does, it's called the Bible."

Meanwhile, Lezah made it through her sophomore year. During her high school days, she always managed to land a job during the summer. She worked at the summer camps within the district helping with the younger children. It was a way to keep her busy while keeping a little change in her pocket. I was very happy with her initiative and ambition. One thing I could never do is accuse my fav daughter of being lazy. With that being said, if I remember correctly, ever since she could talk she always said she was going to college. I was always fascinated with that because it's not something I ever forced on her, but at the same I'm glad the desire was always in her heart. Although she struggled academically, she maintained her stance regarding college and that made me proud. It also showed me her character and how against all odds she was going to put her best foot forward and show the world I can do all things through Christ that strengthens me. (Her favorite scripture).

During her high school days we continued to travel. We took several vacations. We visited Las Vegas, again, which she could appreciate much more. We also visited California and Atlanta. We went to Palm Springs which was too hot and San Diego where the weather was perfect. Oh, how we loved San Diego. During the Christmas season we went to Atlanta to visit her godparents where she was given the royal treatment. Furthermore, on her 16th birthday we went to Boston to see the Celtics play because that was her favorite basketball team at the time. We strived to provide her with many learning experiences through traveling while having fun.

Amazingly, Lezah turned everything around academically during her junior year in high school. She matured in so many ways, particularly, in her work habits, study habits and disciplining herself to achieve better. During her junior year she enrolled in Votech.

Enrolling in the vocational school allowed her to attend high school in the morning and attend classes across town where she was enrolled in the criminal justice program in the afternoon. What a great idea. I personally think all schools should give their students the option of attending a vocational school. This affords them the opportunity to learn a trade such as, mechanics or culinary arts, and also prepare them for college if they choose to attend.

Lezah learned so much and was able to apply herself as well as adjust to the rigorous routine which prepared her for not only her senior year in high school, but also for college. She became more confident within herself and was an honor student for the first time and held onto that title throughout her junior and senior years. Believe me when I say "I was a proud mama." I don't say it bragging, on the contrary, I say it humbly because I know her struggles. I know from where she came. I know it was a long road and others have said "she was a late bloomer." However, I know God answers prayer. God has our Lezah – hazeL backwards in the palm of His hands. Another golden nugget I share with her regularly.

We are parents of a senior in high school. Now one of the perks of working in the school Lezah attended was that the parent would have the honor of handing their child the diploma at graduation. Oh, how I was so looking forward to that opportunity. (Pause and hold that thought). Please understand Lezah is not only a senior at the high school in her district she is also a senior at the vocational school Therefore, we have two graduations to look forward to this year.

Senior year was a whirlwind. Finishing college applications that started while she was a junior in high school. OMG!!! Parents just a tidbit regarding college applications they fall on you, not the student and don't get me started about scholarship applications. I used to think applying for a mortgage was the hardest thing I have ever done, but now I have to say filling out college and scholarship applications had me totally frustrated. Perhaps my age had something to do with it. I'm just saying.

Moving on, my fav daughter passed her driver's test during senior year, took driving lessons and got her provisional license so, of course, for Christmas her father bought her a car. This was an exciting, yet, scary time. She was thrilled and, although, I was happy for her and glad I no longer had to chauffer her from here to there I was scared. However, she did fine, considering.

That same year for her 18th birthday, we rented a party bus and sent her and nine of the folks she hung out with to Great Adventure. The weather was a bit overcast that evening but they all agreed the ride in the limo bus was the highlight of the night. We always attempted to do our best to create memorable moments for Lezah over the years. I know both, me, and my husband did not have parents that could afford to buy our first car or rent us a party bus, however, I can assure you I did have a memorable childhood. For us, it was the little things and I hope our fav daughter will remember these moments as well as cherish them. One of the fondest moments from my childhood is that my mom always made Christmas feel special. I grew up in a home with five other siblings. We would all give her a list for Santa Claus with three items written on it and our mom would make it happen. We didn't have much money and material things, but we had unconditional love showered upon us daily. I believe, my husband would say Christmas was special in his home as well. He has often shared stories with me and Lezah about the "shoebox." He, too, had five siblings and his mom would decorate a shoebox and fill it with all kinds of goodies and place one under the tree for each of them along with many other toys, clothes, among other things. Memories are created to share with others and my hope is that Lezah will share these cherished moments with her children and children's children, God willing.

AND THEN THERE WAS DATING.

What can I say about the dating scene? There is a song I dedicated to her entitled "If I Could" by Regina Belle. I wrote this song in a letter which I gave her at the baby shower when she was 3 months old. We also made a video to the words of the song with pictures and presented it to her as a graduation gift from high school. The words are so befitting for times like these to share with children you love. The times she will experience hurt as a result of the first break up. The times when she realize the best friend was not her friend at all. The times that come along with growing pains which are unavoidable. I love this song and I chose to share it with my daughter to let her know although I can't live your life for you, I would if I could. I would do it to try to prevent you from making the same mistakes I did. However, this journey called life teaches us that we all have to go through and every journey is unique and special. My journey is mine. Lezah's journey is hers. The journey will mold you, shape you, build you and break you while developing your character.

Over the course of her high school years, I guess she had a few crushes. But I believe this first boo or boyfriend was the one she was crushing on since 8th grade. However, we met him during her junior year. She came to me and asked if she could go out on her first date. I remember asking if her proposed date was male or female. She answered "male." I went on to ask if he was Black or White. She answered "Black." I further asked "how long have you liked this young man?" I don't remember what she answered to that. I finally asked if she knew whether or not he was a Christian? And she answered, "I think so, and proceeded to tell me his mom goes to church." Then I believe we had a reboot of "the conversation", again. (smiling). I, also, told her I would discuss it with her dad and let her know what we decided.

Needless to say she went on her first date the same week at seventeen. I remember they went to the movies and I can still visualize what they both wore. I was impressed with the fact that he was polite and I remember thinking somebody other than me and her dad is in our daughter's ear. I'm old enough to know no matter how much we talk and the examples we try to set everyone will be their own person in the end. My mom raised five daughters, one son, and she always said we were all different with different needs.

SENIOR MOMENTS.

Surprisingly, senior year seemed to have gone by quickly. I guess because there were so many things to prepare for. Lezah continued to maintain good grades. She had many deadlines to meet regarding different courses. She was preparing for prom, while deciding what school she would attend. The big decision was whether to attend a four year school or a community college. We decided on a two year community college wherein she would earn her associates degree and finish up at a four year college to earn her bachelor's degree.

In the midst of making decisions about college we were searching for prom dresses. That was an exciting adventure. It was fun hanging with my daughter going here, there and everywhere, looking for dresses. We searched and searched until we both agreed on a gorgeous navy blue gown which fit like a glove. She complimented the dress with silver shoes, a beaded silver purse and matching jewelry. This truly was a busily interesting season for us all.

In the meantime, can we backtrack for a second to where I advised you all to hold the thought about me looking forward to handing my daughter her diploma. Well, the high school she attended has the prom and graduation back to back. (Don't ask). Prom is on Monday and graduation is on Wednesday of the same week. So this is the sad situation, the mom of Lezah's date for prom and I, planned to go together to the florist to pick out the corsage and the boutonniere that Saturday before the main event. A few hours before we were to meet up, my husband and I were cleaning out the TV room in our home. While cleaning, I decided to take an old VCR out of the room and transport it down to the basement. As I was walking down the steps to the basement all I remember at this point is sitting on the step, glancing at my right foot and it was facing all the way to the right. Yes, apparently I had dropped the VCR on my foot and broke it. Meanwhile, I never felt any pain, however, the sight alone caused me to scream, which caused my daughter to scream and my husband too. We were all screaming. I couldn't move. I could hear my daughter on her phone calling my sisters. My husband was on his phone calling the paramedics and my daughter's boyfriend's mother had arrived and was totally confused.

As a result of the fall, I was in a wheelchair with a boot for the prom pics and the graduation. The day of the prom, we had family over and had a prom/graduation celebration combined. I had the food catered, plenty to drink and wrapped thank you gifts. We were all celebrating Lezah's accomplishments while waiting for her to come downstairs fully dressed and made up. Our family and close friends were all in attendance. My favorite daughter was absolutely gorgeous as she sashayed down the stairs to greet us. She and her date, who, was equally as stunning made an attractive couple. The cameras were flashing while everyone was telling her how gorgeous she looked giving her all kinds of advice as the limo pulled up. She came home around midnight feeling good about the evening expressing how fab the night was. I had the opportunity over the years to chaperone a few of the proms (not this one of course) and it's a great place for our students to go to have a fancy time and feel like a grownup. The food is extraordinary, lined up around three walls with everything young folks like from soup to nuts. The ball room is exquisite. The DJ is normally dope. They have a sitting area where you can just chat it up while eating. They have a room with a fireplace that is comfy and cozy. There is a foyer where you can sit and gaze outside at a beautifully decorated patio. In the foyer they have folks cooking hotdogs and burgers on a grill. Really, the young folks have so many choices regarding food and where they wish to hangout. I love the banquet hall and from my understanding, this has been the spot for the prom well before I started working in the district and I have been here close to twelve years. Anyway, Lezah and her date changed clothes and went to New York to an after party celebration. All went well as she continued to make her last high school memories.

We had one day of rest as we anticipated graduation. Due to the fact I was in the wheelchair, the administrator allowed my husband the honor of presenting my daughter with her diploma in my stead. I cannot tell a lie, I was jealous. I had dreamed of that moment for years and I was so looking forward to placing that diploma in her beautiful hands and giving her a big long bear hug to the point she would struggle for me to let her go causing everyone in the audience to laugh. I had played that scenario out over and over and over again in my head. Even though it didn't happen the way I planned it, I trust, know and believe it was the way God purposed it to be. There is something to be said about dads and daughters. As I watched, I remembered how they placed her in his arms (when we picked her up) and she laid her head on his chest and I smiled then and I smiled as he handed our fav daughter her diploma.

Mind you, we are only at the letter "B". Although, most graduations can be boring, because I worked at the school and knew many of these young people that were graduating, this one tended to be a bit more joyous. However, my mind did wander as she walked across the stage. I thought about some of the incidents that made me cry as well as laugh later in life. For instance, when she was about three-years-old she spit on me. Now I know many Black mamas are thinking in their head right now "she spit on you and she had legs to walk across that stage." (laughing). Understand, Lezah and I were attached at the hip. I couldn't move without her. Where I went, she went. If you saw me, Lezah was not far behind. On this particular day I was in the bathroom and I just needed a minute. Normally, I would let her sit on the floor while I took care of my business. But this day, I wanted my privacy and I asked her to let me have a minute and to step out and sit at the door or with her dad. For whatever reason she was not feeling that and the more I insisted, the more anxious she became and then she spit on me. Well, I calmly but firmly stood her straight up (because she was leaning on me the whole time) and looked her right in the eye and instructed her to leave the bathroom. She stomped out. I took care of my business, walked out the bathroom, and snatched her up. Needless to say, my husband had to pull me off of her. I can tell you this much, she never spit on anyone else again thus far in her lifetime.

Oh, we love one another, but we have had our moments. There was a time we were leaving a furniture store, and while we were in the store, she said something smart and when we returned to the car, she got in the backseat. My husband was driving and he proceeded to the front. I opened the door to get in the back with her and I jacked her up. She never saw it coming. Then I thought about an incident, I can't remember exactly how old she was at the time, but, again, this was a day she was giving me a run for my money. I literally fell to my knees, I started praying and asking God, "Father God why does this little girl not listen to me? We feed her, we clothe her, we love her and she just does not listen." I kid you not, those that have ears to hear, will understand when I say I heard the voice of God clearly say to me "that is just one child that does not listen to you, think of all my children who do not listen to me." I got up off my knees and I was hysterically laughing. I have shared that story over the years with other parents because I know we all can relate.

There are many stories I can share. However, the key to parenting is to trust God through the good times and the "so called" bad times. Also, we must understand everything has its purpose. Our children are on loan to us. Ultimately they belong to God. Another golden nugget to pass along.

By the way, about a week or a couple of days later, she had her graduation from Votech and due to the wheelchair and the boot I was unable to make it. However, her dad and then boyfriend, were there to cheer her on. Although the festivities were smaller, she earned another diploma which was equally important to her future endeavors.

While they were gone, I continued to reflect on how God has blessed us over the years.

My fav daughter has come a long way. She has overcome many obstacles. I remember the day I realized she had practically taught herself how to swim. Although I took her to swim lessons at our town pool for a year or more when she was about three or four years old, I never actual saw her swim - until one day we were at the pool when she was, I believe, five at the time. She was watching the older children dive off the diving board and proceeded to tell me she wanted to join. I said "no". She asked "why?" I said "because you don't know how to swim." She insisted with her hand on her hip "Mommy I do know how to swim." After watching or listening to our bantering back and forth, the lifeguard came over and said "that he would follow behind her while in 5" of water and if she can go from one end of the pool to the other then she could dive from the diving board." Well, she did just that, she swam from one side of the pool to the other with no problem and no assistance from the lifeguard. We had the best day ever at the pool while I read my book and kept my eyes on her jumping off the diving board over and over again.

I relived all the basketball games we attended and the excitement of the trophies she received while playing for the community along with all the basketball banquets we shared with the coaches and teammates over the years. Our family was always supportive of Lezah's endeavors.

Then there was Prince. We had the opportunity to take our fav daughter to a Prince concert when she was fifteen. Now I've had the great opportunity to see this amazing entertainer on several occasions. Because of my love for Prince, I wanted Lezah to experience the excitement and the energy of not only Prince but his entire entourage of all those who are blessed to grace the stage with him. I remember in the middle of the concert, as we were dancing in front of our seats, she turned to me and said with excitement in her voice "this is the best concert I ever went to, this is better than Beyonce." That really made my night because we weren't sure how she was going to react. As we drove home, Prince was the topic of our conversation. We sang all the songs while trying to decide which was whose favorite. We narrowed it down to we love all his music!!! Prince can't do any wrong!!! Expectantly, this was the same reaction I had after witnessing the purple one for the first time even before he was this famous. Furthermore, a full size poster (which we purchased that evening) of him still drapes the wall of her bedroom.

LIFE IS GOOD.

Technically, we now have a young lady living with us. She will be nineteen this year going off to college. What a ride this has been. It has been a beautiful ride with its share of bumps in the road. However, God was with us and He walked us around and lifted us over every bump along the way. We take nothing for granted. God is amazing. Thank You, God.

Over the summer we shared family time. Lezah landed a job with the YWCA, which she was happy about because she was no longer working within the school. She had a job with more grown up responsibilities and better pay. This position helped her to build confidence and taught her how to work as a team. The children loved her and the parents were grateful for her, which they demonstrated with lovely thank you tokens at the end of the summer.

The season was also a time for my husband and I to ponder when we would tell Lezah about her birth mother. We had discussed it on several occasions and understood there was no "so called" right time. However, we agreed it would be sometime after her high school graduation. Now the plan had been to wrap the book/album we received from the agency on the day we made our family complete. We planned to give her the album as a gift and then if she had questions we would try our best to answer them to the best of our ability.

Understandably, before I go any further I must add a caveat; I believe I shared earlier that the adoption agency advised us to tell our daughter she was adopted. I also shared that she always knew. As a result, I'm sharing the words of the poem my sister/her godmother gave her, which hangs on her wall in her bedroom, along with a picture of a beautiful angel with wings, the poster of Prince and a poster of the Harlem Globe Trotters. It reads:

Legacy of an Adopted Child

Once there were two women who never knew each other
One you do not remember, the other you call Mother.
Two different lives shaped to make you one.
One became your guiding star, the other became your sun.
The first gave you life and the other taught you to live it.
The first gave you a need for love, the second was there to give
it.
One gave you a nationality, the other gave you a name.
One gave you a talent, the other gave you aim.
One gave you emotions, the other calmed your fears.
One saw your first sweet smile, the other dried your tears.
One sought for you a home that she could not provide,
 the other prayed for a child and her hope was not denied.
And now you ask me through your tears,
 the age old question, unanswered through the years.
Heredity or environment, which are you a product of?
Neither my darling. Neither.
Just two different kinds of Love.

Although the author is anonymous, clearly he or she gets
it. The poem confirms relationships are built on love. Simply
said, I wanted Lezah to know that her birth mother loved her
while she was growing inside her womb and her actions to
allow another couple to raise her were driven by love.

41

GOD LEAD.

Remember, I also shared how she reacted at four years old when she asked me if she came from my womb. With all that in mind during her freshman year in high school she kinda sorta (as the young people would say) started slacking off with homework and study habits. When I addressed this situation with her face to face, she said to me "it was because she didn't have any parents." Now needless to say I handled this much different than when she was four-years-old. First and foremost, I believe I might have said a few swear words. Then I proceeded to say "you have two parents who love you unconditionally. You have aunties, uncles, godparents and many others who love you and are here for you every step of the way. God put this family together, therefore, you will not use the fact that you don't know who your birth parents are as an excuse for not excelling in school. You will not!!!" Now prior to this incident, on occasion, she would ask me about her birth mother and or birth siblings and I would tell her I didn't know who or where they were, but I always reassured Lezah that her birth mother did what she did out of love. However, after that conversation she never mentioned her birth parents again.

So here I am, in a boot, unable to sleep upstairs in my bedroom because I cannot go up and down the stairs. So while I was recuperating, once my husband and daughter would go upstairs to sleep, I had plenty of time to think and decide how we were going to share this album regarding her birth mom and allow her to decide what she wanted to do with this information. I had time to pray and talk to God. In the meantime, I did have her birth mom's telephone number because over the years I looked her up on line. I had her number in my wallet and I decided to put her number in my phone and I took a picture of Lezah's graduation picture and I forwarded I to her with the caption "our girl graduated" or either "she made it." I sent it as information because I do believe if I was in her position I would want to know that the child I gave birth to was doing well. I didn't get a response, but I was okay with that. Again, if I was in her position, how would I respond?

In the meantime, I continued to pray and trust God to lead. In the beginning of August that summer I got my boot off and was told I could drive and of course, I was thrilled. As a result, I invited my fav daughter out for a pedicure, manicure and lunch. While at the mall eating lunch, I felt the need to have a discussion regarding her birth mother. During the discussion, I asked if she would want to meet her. She hesitated and then hinted she didn't think so because she didn't think her dad would be on board.

I told her that I believed he would be okay because we talked about it. I let her know we would 100% support whatever decision she chose to make. Then I went on to tell her that I did have her phone number if she wanted me to reach out to test the waters. To my surprise, she answered, "I want to call her." I said, "you want to call her?" She responded "yes, I want to call her." So, reluctantly, I gave her the number. I say reluctantly, because Momma Mode kicked in. Every mother is going to do everything to protect her child from unnecessary hurt or pain. However, during my prayer time God brought to my attention the fact that neither my husband nor me, could ever know exactly how an adopted person feels. I believe there is a void that only God can fill. I always prayed God would fill that void, however, if this was someone she needed to see face to face I was not going to be the one who prevented that from happening.

As she got up from the table and walked away, tears welled in my eyes and I prayed, "Father God have thine own way." Shortly afterward she returned to the table with a look of dismay and asked if that was the right number. I said "yes." She asked "are you sure?" I said "yes." Then she went on to say that whoever answered the phone denied being her birth mother. My heart sank. I looked my daughter in the eyes and said "trust me that is the correct number. Perhaps she needs sometime to process the information." She gave me back the number and walked away. I yelled out "do you want me to keep the number or throw it away?" She answered with tears in her eyes "keep it."

Momma Mode was in full gear at this point. I got up from the table, walked outside, found a bench to sit on and called the number. The phone rang, I'm thinking she better answer, and she did. I said, "hello, this is Lezah's mom, the young lady that just reached out to you. Please listen to me carefully, you don't have to acknowledge her or deal with her. But what you won't do is have her think I gave her the wrong number because as her mother I would not have given my daughter the number if I was not certain of who it belonged to. Lezah is the answer to both me and my husband's prayers. We love her and she has plenty of folks around us who love her too. I went on to inform her that the only thing I expect from you is to let her know about her bioloical sister and brother because they are close in age and God forbid she could possibly meet and date one of them. Now out of respect for all involved I'm not going to share the rest of the conversation other than, the fact that she, too, prayed and asked God to find her baby a loving, caring home with stability. I will say the conversation was civil and lasted over thirty minutes.

Furthermore, when I met up with my daughter, she was on the phone with her birth mother and before we got home from the mall she had spoken with her birth grandmother and her biological sister. Only God!!!

Within days she was introduced via phone to her birth great grandmother, her birth father and his wife. I was grateful for the positive reaction. Don't get me wrong I am happy the response went well. However, I was concerned because you don't know people until you get to know people. Therefore, I advised her to inhale, exhale, breathe and slowly take it all in.

In the meantime, a few weeks after talking to her birth mom on the phone, they set up a date to meet face to face. She came to the house on a Sunday after church and she and I, along with my husband sat and talked for about thirty minutes. I was glad we had spoken over the phone prior to the visit because it helped break the ice. We exchanged hugs, which gave us a sense of ease. After the pleasantries, we all felt comfortable and she and Lezah went on their date. Upon their return from the date, she came in and we talked some more. We shared pictures of different events. Overall, when she left I had a level or comfort. More importantly, I believe Lezah felt good about the entire situation. Again, my job as a mother is to make my child feel whole. My desire was for whatever void needing to be filled would be filled.

For her upcoming birthday (the 19th) she asked if both families could come together. Lezah's idea for the birth mom and her family, birth dad and his family, along with both sides of our family to come together was her true wish. We also extended the invitation to some of our closest friends and her godparents. At first I wasn't sure. Of course, I ran it by my husband and siblings. I don't think any of us were sure about it. However, we complied for Lezah's sake. Again, whatever it takes to fill the void. We reached out to a caterer for the food. My niece decorated the house beautifully. Our fav daughter was a bit nervous and excited. The evening came, and everyone showed up. The food was delicious, the conversation was intriguing and surprisingly we all got along. We laughed, we cried (tears of joy), shared stories, hugged and embraced one another with the love of God. We took loads of pictures making memories along with a video. Often times, we can pre-judge a situation and I know some of my family came ready to not get along, however, the opposite happened. Understandably, when God is in the mix all things work out according to His will.

Meanwhile, we had to accept the fact that Lezah's family had grown. She gained two siblings on her birth mother's side and she gained 3 or 4 siblings on her birth father's side. Not for nothing those can be questionable. Can I just be real? The plus in my eyes was the fact she got to know a host of cousins around her same age which was great for her social life. They started right off the bat hanging out, going to movies, parties and having sleepovers until a little miss step that ended in a big argument and a near physical altercation. As I stated you don't know people until you know people. I'm happy to say overtime things worked themselves out and everyone is good. When you are between the ages of 16 and 24 things can be unpredictable regardless of the circumstances. The fact that Lezah grew up the only child, she had to adjust to the many variables that came with the situation. I know for sure she was excited about the relationship with both her birth brother and sister and those two relationships continued to bloom.

By the way, did I mention that her great-grandmother (who recently passed) on her birth mom's side name was also Hazel? Who knew? Her name connects her to both families – Lezah – hazeL backwards.

Meanwhile, we got through the summer of 2015 ending with an unexpected bang by meeting all the new found family. This time required her to develop new relationships while trying to process the emotional aspects of them all. I couldn't help but wonder "what exactly is she feeling?" I know we can't always put every feeling and emotion into words. Therefore, during this time I continued to pray and trust God.

OFF TO COLLEGE.

Through it all, Lezah was preparing for her first year of college. She commuted by car Monday through Thursday. Although she was nervous at first, she navigated the system. She made friends, enjoyed her weekends and acclimated herself pretty well. She joined the Black Student Union and was very instrumental in getting the organization charted. It was not an easy feat. Nevertheless, our fav daughter, along with others, did not give in to the push back. They remained focused and determined. In my eyes, that was a big deal and her dad and I were extremely proud of the role she played in accomplishing her academic endeavor.

During this time, her relationship with her birth mother and birth family continued to blossom. However, her relationship with her boyfriend at the time was on shaky ground. If my memory serves me correctly, they broke up for good early January 2016. There had been some mishaps over the course of their relationship, however, this was the finale. I have to say I was saddened because my husband and I both had become friends with his parents. We had several couple's nights out. We broke bread together on many occasions, went to see plays and concerts. I can honestly say, we enjoyed each other's company. I have to admit we were warned by others that perhaps this was not a good idea (getting too friendly) because of the ages of our children and relationships come and go. I remember telling one of her godparents, after I broke my ankle, that even if Lezah and her boo didn't make it, his parents were keepers. This family was very attentive during my recoup time and was there to help me through the healing process. Not only that, I believed we had created a bond. Although it didn't work out the way I had hoped, I will be forever grateful for the roll they played in our lives. I realized it would be hard for me to maintain a relationship with anyone who disrespects my fav daughter. To be fair, they probably felt the same way about their favorite son. In hindsight, I must admit their relationship was toxic and the adults (his mom and I) were too involved. With that being said, I genuinely care about the entire family. To this day, I keep them prayed up and reach out to the mom every so often to check in. Life teaches us lessons. People come into your life for a reason and/or a season. The key is to learn from the lessons and cherish the memories that were made.

Let me share a golden nugget with dads. There were times during my daughter's relationship with her boyfriend she would get down and out because something may have happened that pissed her off. Words would be said. A breakup ensued prior to a makeup. However, with this final breakup I had expected her to be down for a few days, but she wasn't. I approached her and asked "why she was handling this breakup differently?" She proceeded to tell me that it was because her dad sat her down and discussed with her "her worth." She said "he never mentioned the other person's name once." It was all about her and who she is and who she had the potential to become. It was about her going off to school and preparing for the next chapter of her life. He instilled in her that she is somebody and the importance of not allowing another human being to define you. I was extremely pleased with the fact that her dad took the time to speak life over her and the fact that she received it, kept smiling and kept it moving.

Furthermore, she was doing her thing throughout her first two years in college. She was dating again. She was the chairperson for a trip to the Schoenberg Center in New York. During her sophomore year, she placed her name on the ballot to run for class president. She was also awarded with a certificate for Sociology Student of the year. My fav daughter made strides during her two years at community college and graduated with a GPA we were all proud of. With every accomplishment and hurdle she was able to overcome, I reminded her of who God is and to trust Him through it all. It was during the graduation ceremony wherein she earned her Associates Degree that I realized my daughter was determined to defy all the odds; despite the fact she was not raised by her birth mom; despite the fact she was classified with a learning disability; despite the fact she was bullied; despite the fact she struggled internally; she was determined (and still is) to absorb, learn, grow and push forward no matter what. I love her for her tenacity. I love her because of her resilience. I love her because she is doing things on her terms with purpose. I love her because God loves her and He has bestowed His love upon her and within her. I am happy she was able to meet her birth mother and family. The encounter may have helped in ways I may never fully realize. However, there is a void that only God and the love of God can fill. I thank Him every single day for hearing my cries and answering my prayers and blessing our home with the pitter patter of little feet whom we call Lezah – hazeL backwards.

We are at graduation number four. We have sat through middle school, high school, Votech and now community college. You all should know by now this is the time I reflect on things that happened over the years. As we sat with our friends whose daughter also was graduating with Lezah, we, together, reflected on the years they spent together in my daycare. Their friendship began while they were toddlers. They also attended the same middle school and high school. We reflected on the playdates they shared and the two birthday parties they shared (the 10th and the 13th). The church events were memorable, particularly the roles they played in the Toms Thumb Wedding. The concerts, I remember Lezah singing America the Beautiful during a concert at church and totally knocked it out to the park. She never ceases to amaze us when she puts her mind to something. We were ready to send her off to voice lessons with hopes of her becoming the next Whitney. (laughing). Nonetheless, that was not her plan. We all went to Disney World together. Yes, this family and ours have shared many memorable moments over the years.

I thought of the all the people who were instrumental in shaping her path. I may have not agreed with her teachers all the time, however, every teacher appreciation week they received a note of thanks. She was surrounded by professionals, laymen and Christians who truly cared about her academics. My siblings, her beautiful aunties, on both sides of the family, were always ready and willing to pour into her whenever needed. She may not have always liked it (what was being said) but she knew the importance of showing respect. There may have been one or two incidents when she went off track, but believe me she immediately got reigned in. I instilled in her the importance of finding someone to talk with if she could not talk to her dad or me.

Young people need a safe haven. The last thing we want is for our children to have stuff bottled up inside and nowhere to turn. I appreciate her older cousins who made themselves available to take her here or there when I had something important to do. It truly does take a village. I am grateful for my village, because from day one they made Lezah feel welcomed as well as special. I love my family, friends and those God has placed in our path over the years.

In March, of the same year of her graduation, she was accepted into Rowan College. My Fav daughter is going places. We had an intimate celebration party prior to her attending classes in the fall. This party was for her friends and of course, her aunties showed up. The three of us wore our Rowan t-shirts. It was all good. They hung out at our house until around midnight and they (the young folks) took the celebration to another venue. However, in the midst of the party we learned how small the world is because her best (male) friend from the community college mom is friends with two of her aunties. He's a nice young man who she could hang out with and bounce things off of. We were happy to learn about their friendship. She would often mention his name and I assumed it was a crush, but it turned out it was a good friendship. Over the years, I find male friends can be an asset to a young ladies' maturing. Male/female relationships can bring a different perspective to a conversation that allows both genders to reflect and examine a situation in another light.

That summer, she continued to work at the summer camp housed in the Y, maintaining positive relationships with the young people she adored and vice versa. Of course, she got her party on with friends. Oh, and the guy she was dating has now become her new boyfriend.

In the meantime, she was anxious about attending a four year college while looking forward to living on campus. She was concerned about who her roommate would be and whether or not they would get along. Fortunately, when she received her assigned room, she did not have a roommate at the time. However, she knew anything could happen before move in day.

Once we received the information regarding move in, we proceeded to go shopping for the essentials for her room. My living room was filled with boxes. We ordered linens, bedding, toiletries, and packed a medical emergency kit. We purchased a computer, television, microwave and everything else that was allowed. While this is another exciting chapter in Lezah's life, it's also a costly time for mom and dad. Sidebar: College is expensive and we need to make college more affordable for our children and parents. I don't want to think about what her children and grand's will have to pay.

As move in day approached, I wondered how I was going to handle Lezah living away from home. Although the college was only one hour and fifty minutes away, I was still apprehensive. I want to believe that her dad and I raised her right, but right for us may not be right for her. I realized through it all, I have to trust God.

We packed up both cars with the help of her boyfriend who was definitely a tremendous help. His dad operates a moving company, therefore, he was able to share his expertise in packing and handling the items. Once the cars were packed, we began our journey up the highway. I had time to reflect, ponder and consider all that was going on. My mind was racing for whatever reason. I guess I was happy as well as nervous. My daughter, my favorite daughter, my only daughter, would be sleeping away from home for the next two years and I had to adjust. I had to accept the fact that Glassboro, New Jersey, will be her temporary home. However, "temporary" is the key word here and at that moment the word gave me solace.

As we arrived to our destination, I said to her dad "I do love this campus." Move in day was very busy. Cars were lined up ahead of us. Soon we were motioned to a parking space, given directions as to where to go and what to do. We watched others hustle and bustle with their children and it dawned on me that folks have been going to and from college for years. This is not a new phenomenon, get it together mom.

After waiting for the one elevator we all used to go up and down, we finally brought all her things up to her room. Whew, that was a relief! Now we had the task of unpacking and setting everything up. I had to remind myself to let her have the final say as to what goes where. It's her space and she was happy when she heard she would not have a roommate this winter semester. Luckily, it turned out she was solo the spring semester as well. This gave her a real sense of maturity and when she traveled home, I witnessed the growth first hand. She still could have kept her room cleaner, however, I was grateful for the ability to hold a conversation with her, listen and consider one another's feelings without any tension.

I'm almost embarrassed to admit that after about two weeks of her being away from home I got used to the idea. I did toss and turn the first couple of nights. Thereafter, I found my comfort zone. Her dad and I had time for ourselves. The house was tidy. We didn't have to take time to maneuver cars in the morning prior to going off to work. Please, don't get me started about the quiet. I love quiet. I love to relax. There is something to be said about young adults living in the house, there is always something going on. They are in and out all times of the night. They leave the house and forget to lock the door behind them or put the alarm on. They come home and you think they are in for the night and then they are gone again or have to go to the car and get this or that. God forbid if they can't charge their phone or can't listen to music through their ear buds. Mind you, we have a chime on our door so every time someone comes in or out the chime sounds. No need to say anything else. Anyways, these past two years of her living between campus and home has been interesting. However, it confirmed that after a certain age young adults need their own space. Therefore, going forward my prayer is that she earn her degree, land a good paying job, and rent an apartment that comes with a maid.

Lezah continued to thrive academically. The first year of her enrollment at a four-year school went well. We were all pleased with how she faired both semesters. We realized attending community college and earning an associate's degree was an excellent choice financially, academically and socially. With the associate's degree under her belt, she had a leg up on acquiring an internship not far from campus, allowing her the ability to witness first-hand the life of a social worker. She managed to keep her grades up, get through her finals, make friends and lose some all in the name of becoming a grown up. As I type these words, a light bulb went off "I get it." The title of our former first lady's book, *Becoming* is the perfect word to describe the roads we travel, the daily challenges we face and the maturation process. As long as we have breath in our bodies we are becoming. That was a defining "Ah ha" moment. Thank you, First Lady Michelle Obama for sharing your journey with us.

Meanwhile, before we knew it, the junior/third year of college was behind us. Now we have the privilege of experiencing move out day. Forget the cost of college for a second, it also takes work. Packing, unpacking, making sure the room is clean and praying we don't receive a bill for this or that. We did end up paying $35 for a missing extension cord. I guess we were lucky.

That summer, she continued with her usual job of working at the "Y" with the little ones. This year, she was a lead counselor which afforded her an increase in salary along with more managerial responsibilities. She handled it. However, the damper, that summer, was she got an infection in her teeth which required her to get her four wisdom teeth pulled at the same time. My poor baby underwent oral surgery. Oh my God, I felt so bad for her. That song "If I Could" (which I mentioned earlier) came to life. Awakening from the anesthesia was hilarious. That young lady was too funny, talking all kinds of mess and even swearing. I have video to back it up. She managed to pull through with the least amount of pain killers. The last thing I wanted was for my young lady to get hooked on opioids. I took full control of the situation and was very happy she was in full agreement. We have heard many stories of how one can get hooked on these pain killers. We followed the doctor's instructions and she was healed and eating within five days. Before she returned back to work, she managed to get a mini summer vacation in. Now off to her senior year at Rowan.

The senior year of college seems to have gone by very quickly. Perhaps not for Lezah, but I felt graduation day approached quickly. She was excited about the fact that she would be moving into an apartment on campus. These apartments came with two baths, six bedrooms, a full kitchen and a living room. The draw back for her dad and me was the fact that her roommates were made up of male and female students. We didn't particularly like the idea of her living with young men. However, she reassured us that she was okay with the idea because everyone had a key to their own bedrooms which were normally locked. She was confident that shared living space would come with ground rules and everyone would be respectful towards one another. I was surprised when she agreed to the living arrangement because I know my daughter. She likes her space and growing up an only child, sharing takes work. Now that she is an adult and had lived alone her first year while on campus, I didn't think this scenario was going to suit her. However, she managed to get through it. She didn't really make friends with the other roommates and there were a few run-ins, but she survived them.

The most exciting aspect of her senior year was her trip to India with the education department. That truly was a big deal for all of us. She came home one weekend and told us she had heard the education department was going to India in January 2019. She shared with us that she was going to reach out to the department to inquire as to whether or not she could travel with the group. However, she wasn't sure they would say yes because she is not an education major. From her first day of college, she always expressed the desire to travel abroad and this was a great opportunity to fulfill that desire. Meanwhile, she reached out to the person who sponsored the trip for the past three years and to our surprise he said "yes."

We immediately began to share the good news with family and friends. We set up a GoFundMe Page. The trip cost $4000 and we managed to raise $2000 which was a great help to us. The money was due around the middle week of December 2018. Therefore, we were able to pay off the trip and buy her all the essentials for the trip and gave them to her for Christmas presents. That was a great Christmas for a twenty-two-year old. I'm just saying. We bought her a journal, camera, an apple watch, pajamas, under garments and outfits that included cargo pants. According to her, these were all the things she couldn't live without during her stay in India.

The sponsor setup email accounts between the students and all the parents for correspondence purposes. We all joined his Facebook page so we could see pictures. We were encouraged to get a specific phone plan so the phone calls would not be so expensive. Overall, I was pleased that the trip was planned out very well.

We got through the Christmas break and New Year's Eve. Finally, January 5, 2019, departure day arrived. Her dad was very careful to pack her bag according to the instructions of the airlines to avoid paying extra money. We were all excited while driving to the airport. When we arrived, we hooked up with the other families and sponsor. The sponsor handed out matching tee shirts for them to wear when they visited the schools. We took pictures and the students moved through the gate as the parents waved goodbye. The flight was twenty-three hours with a layover in Mumbai. I was relieved when she called during the layover and even more relieved when she sent a message they had arrived in India safely. I was very happy to hear her voice on the phone from the other side of the world. I asked her how the flight went and she stated "I was really nervous flying over such a large body of water." Other than that, she was okay. The sponsor made sure he posted pictures every single day on Facebook. It was a relief to see Lezah and the other students enjoying another country. The pictures were amazingly beautiful. I couldn't believe the hotels that they stayed in were all five star. The purpose of the trip was to communicate and share with younger students in schools located in some of the deprived areas in India. They managed to serve their purpose. They were responsible for bringing items to share with the children. Lezah brought stickers, notebooks and small frames for the many pictures she would take with her camera. Even with all the attention focused on the students, they managed to get sight- seeing in. They rode camels, had dinner with a native couple allowing them to taste the authentic Indian cuisine, and visited the Taj Mahal amongst other things. They also slept overnight in tents. I understand that was an experience, but it turned out better than they had anticipated it would be.

The India trip was a hit. She was of service to young folks in another country. She made friends and they still remain in touch. She had the privilege to experience another culture. Upon her arrival from the long flight home, we learned she had a hiccup at the airport. A hiccup is putting it mildly. However, I advised her to not concentrate on one negative aspect when you had so many other beautiful experiences. I decided not to give it a place on the pages of this book. I'll just say racism exists all over the world.

We are at the last semester of school before receiving a BA of Science degree. I really can't believe the matriculation of four years of college is about to come to an end. We have accomplished another milestone accompanied by another diploma. I say "we" because we are all in this together. We, meaning, her dad and I, aunties, uncles, cousins, godparents and every person that has poured into her over the years. When I think of the time, money and hard work we put into education, you would think this country would do better by our young people. The job market is getting scarce. I pray hard for this country and for our future with regard to our young people. In the meantime, Lezah decided to continue her education by applying to grad school to obtain her master's degree in social work. Understand my desire is for her to get a job. However, her dad agrees she should continue her education because they (the powers that be) have set the bar higher for us. Therefore, she proceeded to apply to Hunter College in New York, Rutgers, and Kean both in New Jersey to pursue her master's degree.

One day while sitting at work, I receive a phone call. Lezah sounds like she is crying, excited and scared all rolled up into one. I'm panicking on the other end of the line and afraid to ask "what's wrong?" However, I did ask. "What's going on? Are you okay?" She replied "Mommy, Mommy, Mommy, I got in, I got into Hunter." I was relieved, however, I replied, "girl you can't call me like this at work. All excited but sounding more upset then excited. You are about to give me a heart attack." After calming down, and both of us caught our breath I congratulated her and thanked God for everything He has allowed her to accomplish in this lifetime. We texted my husband the good news. He was elated and offered congratulations.

We all agreed getting into Hunter was a challenge. I remember the day she had the initial interview. She was excited and nervous. She dressed appropriately. She caught the train and started on her way. Upon her return back to Jersey, she called me and reported step by step what took place. She was certain she nailed the verbal (face-to-face) interview, however, she wasn't quite sure about the written portion. In the meantime, we waited patiently and a few weeks later she received the phone call, email and then the official letter which started out Dear Lezah, "You have been accepted into Hunter's two year program, etc." She was also accepted into Kean's program and we found out later she had passed the deadline to apply to Rutgers. She chose Hunter.

Now the question is "how do we pay for it?" My husband and I prided ourselves in doing our best to avoid her having an outstanding student loan bill after college. I must say "we achieved that." (Thank God). Therefore, we let her know that for these two years she would have to apply for a loan. She did and next stop – Hunter.

This semester is about to come to an end. I must say I am extremely proud of Lezah. All while preparing for final projects and exams, she is applying for summer jobs. She also mentioned becoming an Uber driver. I attempted to put my foot down on that one because there is too much going on. I barely want her to take an Uber let alone drive for them. I expressed my concerns and put that idea on the back burner for now. In the meantime, she was hired at a retail store at one of the malls and obtained a babysitting position as well. The position at the store started a week prior to graduation. She literally worked every day leading up to the day before the ceremony. That left her one day to get herself all beautified by getting her hair, nails and feet done.

Every graduation/moving up ceremony from pre-school to now were exciting times. Each occasion was momentous. However, Saturday, May 11, 2019, I'm feeling extremely proud. The college she attended has two ceremonies. Of course Lezah decided she would attend both ceremonies, which means her dad and I will also attend both. Saturday's ceremony was the big one held on the football field with the guest speaker and the entire class of 2019. It was an overcast day and we were praying God would hold back the rain. He did for the most part, but we did experience light rain for about three to five minutes and I remember a gentleman sitting directly in back of me stated "it's okay, God is blessing the children." I thought that was a pleasant way to look at it. The graduation was absolutely amazing. The speaker spoke well. There were a lot of positive messages relayed to the graduates and Miss Lezah's face was all over the jumbotron. I guess there are advantages to your last name beginning with "B" and you get to sit on the front row. I found myself paying more attention to the words being spoken than daydreaming. Then a scripture played over and over in my head; Jeremiah 29:11 which reads "For I know the plans I have for you, declares the Lord, plans to prosper you and not to harm you, plans to give you hope and a future." As usual, I thanked God for this day, and for allowing her another opportunity to witness firsthand how good God is.

After the ceremony, we took loads of pictures. We were joined by two of her aunts, an uncle, her boyfriend and his mom. Later, we traveled to Philly to a restaurant. It was very noisy, but the food and drinks were good and we just doted on the graduate. The graduate continued to celebrate through Tuesday, partying with friends, other graduates from different schools and other family members.

Tuesday's celebration was a smaller gathering for those in the same concentrated field. The plus in having the two ceremonies allowed most of the family members to attend one or the other. Unfortunately, we had a forecast for rain on Tuesday as well. Although it didn't rain, the administrators moved the ceremony into the gym. Since the ceremony was moved, we had to shorten the guest list. Many of her friends made their way in, living on campus they knew how to maneuver. However, the family members were her dad, her birth mom and birth grandmother and me. Due to the circumstances, the ceremony wasn't as festive and we watched parts of it on a screen, which they live streamed from another gym. Needless to say Lezah was a little disappointed. Nevertheless, we got through it. Following the ceremony, we took more pictures. She was smiling and relieved. Stating, "I made it." "Whew, now I can enjoy my summer." She had invited more family and friends to join her later at a restaurant. Dad and I are glad you made it and happy you can enjoy your summer, however we have decided to sit this one out. I thought, "it is time for us to just breathe!!!

JUST BREATHE.

As we drove home, we reminisced about both graduations and discussed how far our daughter has come. We realized it has been a challenge. Parenting has its ups and downs and its in-betweens. However, we know God gave us the strength and the wisdom to stop, breathe and pray Lezah and us through it all. We remembered all her special moments from the first time we laid eyes on her. We thought of the times when she was just a baby her dad lifted her up in his arms and flew her all around the room traveling to Kuga Monga, a made up village in Africa. That visual put a smile on my face because I loved to watch him do that with her and she would crack up laughing the entire time. The innocence of a baby/toddler laughing is one of my favorite sounds to hear. I also used to love watching her lay her head on his chest while napping together on the couch. We reflected on the songs we used to sing to her from the hymnal, trusting the lyrics would resonate throughout her little body and give her peace. The thought that makes me tear up a little is of the times I would get up in the wee hours of the morning and would hear her whimpering in her sleep. I remember consulting with her doctor and he responded it could possibly be separation anxiety (as a result from leaving her biological mother's womb). However, I began to pray over her whenever I heard it and one day it dawned on me that it had stopped. I love how God just intervenes on our behalf.

We have so many beautiful memories I could share, however, I believe some stories are for her to tell from her own perspective. Perhaps she will be inspired to write a book. In the meantime, I'm looking forward to what God has in store for her in the future. I told her recently "dad and I have done what God has required of us. Now it is up to you to set goals and initiate a plan." One year I sent her off to school with a bag with a quote that read "be the change you want to see in the world." She loves quotes. I'm believing, praying and trusting she will be who God has purposed her to be. I know she will make mistakes, fail and lose sight at some points while on this journey. However, the key is to learn from the mistakes. Always know that nothing beats a failure but a try and we walk by faith and not by sight.

Meanwhile, I encouraged her to enjoy the summer before she tackles grad school. She met with her class advisor at Hunter to go over her schedule for the fall and discuss grad school expectations. She is very excited about the process and is very happy about her accomplishments to date. As stated, she is working two part-time jobs for the summer to keep a little change in her pocket. She continues to hangout on the weekend catching up with friends, while continuously celebrating earning her degree. She is looking forward to her vacation to a beautiful island in August (our graduation gift to her) where she can soak up the sun and relax on the beach getting in some quiet time. It's nothing like white sand and blue/green ocean water to alleviate the stresses of the world.

My advice to my favorite daughter, Lezah, (Hazel backwards) as she approaches the next chapter of life is to "don't let nothing and no one steal your joy." "You can do all things through Christ that strengthens you." "Keep smiling." Finally, when you lose something or someone or just feel like you're lost "STOP, BREATHE AND PRAY..."

CHERISHED MEMORIES.

My daughter wrote a poem while in high school for her Language Arts Class that blessed my heart. The poem was accompanied with the picture. It reads:

Adopted
By Lezah Brown 11/23/14

It was taken
a surprise, maybe?
Beaming like a blazing lightning bolt.
A breath of fresh air
to a family that needed it so.

You can see it in my eyes
curious and captivated
on the plastic chair
ribbon in hair
tiny finger grip the arm
for support like a mother care

I am not their blood
I am their heart.

I wrote this poem for my fave daughter and gave it to her on Mother's Day in 2018. It reads:

A Daughter
A daughter is a wonderful blessing.
A treasure from above.
She's laughter, warmth and has special charm.
She's thoughtfulness and love.

A daughter brings a special joy,
that comes from deep inside.
And as she grows to adulthood,
she fills your heart with pride.

With every year that passes,
she's more special than before.
Through every stage, through every age,
you love her even more.

No words can describe the warm memories,
the proud moments and struggles, too.
That comes from having a daughter,
to love and to cherish…just like you.
To my Fave Daughter, Lezah Imani
I LOVE YOU
From a proud mother on Mother's Day

Conclusion - What's In a Name

Lezah - derived from h a z e l in honor of her grandmother on her dad's side whose name was Hazel (Hazel backwards) whom she never had the opportunity to meet. I know if she had, Grandma Hazel would have spoiled her rotten. Ironically, we later found out (after meeting her birth parents) her great grandmother on her birth mother's side, also, shared the same name linking her spiritually to that side of the family.

Imani - means faith. The scripture reads "faith is the substance of things hoped for and the evidence of things not seen." I testified to my church family how I fully realized what that scripture meant to me after God answered our prayers by blessing our home with the pitter patter of little feet, which were attached to our beautiful baby girl. We couldn't see her or feel her at the time but she was hovering in the atmosphere waiting for us to bring her home claiming her as our own. I could now speak that scripture out loud with confidence because I'm living it. I trust Lezah, too, will realize the true meaning of faith in her life.

Brown - her Father's last name. It's an honor to have someone bless you with their last name which demonstrates their unconditional love toward you. My desire is for her to honor the "Brown" name and wear it proudly until she marries someone who is worthy of replacing it with a new name or adding to it.

I've heard people ask the question what's in a name. A name is important because it speaks life and truth to a person. I must say I was asked (and criticized) why did I name my daughter Lezah – Hazel backwards. However, I have no regrets. I believe it fits her personality and as I stated early on I was paying homage to her grandmother. Hazel means hazel deriving from the tree and color.

The closest name to Hazel in the bible is Haezel (1Kings) which means God sees/has seen. Therefore, I believe Lezah, if it were biblical would mean see God. My sincere prayer for my fav daughter is that she does, will, and continue to see God in every aspect of her life. My hope for her is to see Him in the good and the "so-called bad times." I desire she see God on top of the mountain as well as down in the valley.

My last nugget, after lovingly laboring over this book, I would encourage you to please take time to research the history of your name and if you are one of those people that ask or get asked the question, "what's in a name?' Be prepared to answer with confidence, the meaning and origin of your name. Then own it and wear it well.

Grandma Hazel

H A Z E L

B A C K W A R D S

Michaia Brown

Made in the USA
Coppell, TX
07 February 2021

49825763R10048